meraki

maleeha ravat

© 2021

the wrong words
were always screamed at me.

maybe that's why,
i wanted to learn
how to say the right ones.

first poem i wrote
after i wrote this,
i decided that i need
to write a whole
book

me and you are not the same,
but we have been hurt the same.
by the people who promised us
forever
and for reasons unexplained,
were the first ones to go.

some parts of me and you have
healed.
whilst other parts still pain us,
as if we were broken yesterday.

all we do know is how to love
ourselves.
the way we should've,
and the way we deserved to from
the beginning.

i know where i am,
but my mind drifts away
senselessly.

is that where my heart truly lies,
in that unknown space far away
from you?

of course, i have a purpose,
but is it intertwined with yours?

i can't help thinking our
relationship
is just a mere phase,
leading me to a greater one.

maleeha ravat

i hate this night.
i think it's because you're with
me,
but not completely.

worry covers your face,
like the clouds cover this small
town.

don't smile,
because you don't want to cry.
don't stay quiet,
because you know if you talk,
you'll end up screaming.

by the end of it all,
i accept this night.
because it's just one night
out of many.

maleeha ravat

sometimes, the days seem to drag
and i don't do anything special.

but then i remember,
the fact that i'm still breathing
is nothing less of a miracle.

just like an umbrella,
can't protect you from
every drop of rain.

it goes without saying,
no matter how strong you are,
every now and again,
you will still feel pain.

how long was i supposed to hold
on?
to memories of a person
that never belonged to me.

so like the air that rushes out of
my lungs,
i let you go.

everyone expects me to have an
answer.
but how can i give a reply?
if everyone has been given a
different set of questions,
to deal with in this lifetime.

i am alone,
but weirdly not lonely.

the candle flickers by the
window,
and the moon shoots me smiles
from outside.

it's as if i have everything,
despite having nothing
extraordinary.

in this moment, i am complete.

everything you do speaks for
itself.

don't you realise,
that even your tears are words.

words your heart can't seem to
express yet.

even in the middle of the night,
i find you in the same place,
you were during the day.

your comfort speaks more than
words can.
but then you speak,
and your soft words soothe my
aching heart.

somehow, your fingers are
always tangled with mine.
if you're not with me,
my mind wanders off to thoughts
filled with you.

you are always beside me.

maleeha ravat

after there was just distance left.

i realised that maybe,
we were destined
to be happy separately
and just not
together.

there's so much to say.

but, something is stopping me,
from baring all my heart for you
to see.

if you're right for me.
one day, the hesitation that
lingers
between us
will no longer exist.

i believe it's naive to think the journey
that is written for us,
means we only have to take one path.

we are meant to fall
or get lost.
so we can find a completely new path,
lighting up the way that's truly meant for us.

over time, you realise people
wander into your life
to show you how not to love,
or how a relationship shouldn't
be.

it's a lesson that hurts more than
anything,
but the teachings you are left
with
last a lifetime.

maleeha ravat

happiness is a fleeting state,
and so is sadness.
to experience both,
with a million other emotions
daily,
is typical in life.

even if it's your dream,
you can grow tired of it
or get too comfortable.

in doubtful moments,
you can even question them.

whether you wish to chase those
dreams,
or give them up for reasons
you choose to never share.

remember, just having a dream
in the first place,
that makes you feel all these
emotions,
is beyond remarkable.

like a single bright ray of light,
your warmth caresses my face
slowly.

a smile is painted across my lips
and my eyes met yours
haughtily.

it seems like a lucky blessing,
that i can bask in
your embrace
and your company
for the rest of my life.

being understanding isn't easy.
accepting your mistakes isn't
easy.
facing people you've hurt,
or people that have hurt you isn't
easy.

the right path isn't easy.

maybe, that's why it's the right
path.

they left,
but they still make you question
why.

don't you feel tired?

looking for answers,
from someone who won't even
spare you a glance.

at times, i try too hard to move
forward.
that i have to remind myself,
that my present is precious
and worthy of my attention too.

my eyes have seen a lot.
my heart has felt as much too.

but i truly know my life has yet
to begin.

i have always recognised the
power of words.
i must tread lightly and kindly.

a wrong word could lead to a
wound.

a wound that would eventually
heal up,
but the pain would always
remain a bitter memory.

since you choose not to do the
right thing,
i separated myself from you.
before, you could do the wrong
thing again.

rain soaks my clothes
as memories flood into my mind.

days where we thought our hands
were designed for only each
other.

moments where we considered
ourselves lucky,
as we had each other's shoulders
to cry on.

seconds where we naively
believed,
our laughter would be timeless.

now the storm has stopped.

so has all the pain.

i think i can blossom now.

how can you see past the walls?

these same walls i've
strengthened and spend years
perfecting.

why am i visible to you?

why do you only see the sadness
in my tired eyes?
whilst everyone is convinced
with my fake smiles.

i don't know what i feel?

is what i'm thinking true?

we were meant to cross paths,
not to travel down the same one
together.

but to make us remember,
anyone can get lost.

on those nights that seem too
dark,
i can't help but wonder.

if the decisions that led me to the
place today,
are the ones i should've made.

forever is impossible.
so stay by my side for as long as
you can.

if you somehow leave me first,
know that your love will remain
until i join you.

maleeha ravat

love and time shouldn't be the
reason,
to tie me to a place that i
outgrew.

i feel suffocated.

can't you see?

i don't belong here.

maleeha ravat

taking a step back,
allowed me to see
that you had already taken many.

i guess it was just fate,
that i began wandering away
in the space you created.

would you think of me
differently?
if i told you,
i'm happy they hurt me.

i may have lost things,
but what i've gained
surpasses what is no longer mine.

want and need
are two different things.

but, if people get confused over
love and attachment.

it isn't a surprise,
that they end up
wanting what they don't need.

maleeha ravat

i don't think it's your fault.

maybe, try giving yourself that
endless love
you freely give to others.

my reason is you,
and your reason is me.

now tell me,
how was i not supposed to love
you
with everything in me?

maleeha ravat

i always wanted to do more
because i thought
i was moving slowly
compared to everyone.

but, doing that much more
made me feel like
i wasn't living the way i wanted
to.

so i chose to move at a pace,
that i could wholeheartedly call
my own.

i always wondered,
do oceans like humans
feel so empty,
when they're that full and deep.

of course, you can do it if you
try.

but asking for help,
doesn't make you any less of a
person.
talking about what is worrying
you
or leaning on others for support
is okay for you to do too.

doesn't it get tiring trying to do it
all by yourself?

it's hard, isn't it?
but you're still here.

i'm proud of you for not leaving.

maleeha ravat

when did life move this fast?

it seems like just yesterday,
i had almost given up.

now i look up,
to the same shining stars
that i cried to.

somehow, they twinkle back,
twice as proud.

it was never about being the best,
or even being good.

it was more than enough
if what i was,
was real.

maleeha ravat

i used to scream helplessly,
around those who would cover
their ears
and pretend not to hear.

now, my heart feels so full
being surrounded by people
who know i need comforting
before i even tell them.

maleeha ravat

i know i won't be okay
tomorrow,
or maybe as fast as i'd like to be.

but, before i know it,
i won't remember this pain.

life gets too busy.
if you don't stop
to take a breath
and see where you are.

you may forget
how far you've come
and how far you have to go too.

before being with you,
i need to make sure
i completely belong to myself.

that i belong to my dreams,
mistakes
and impulsive decisions.

otherwise, i will only belong to
regrets.

maleeha ravat

i truly believe that,
courage is picking yourself up,
after you've fallen a little more
harder than last time.

life is changing.

of course, it will.

change is what's promised
with growth.

if this world isn't perfect,
or the people that live on it
aren't,
or even the way people love
isn't.

how can *we* be perfect?

how can *you* be perfect?

how can *i* be perfect?

i want to confess that i feel lost.

i feel lost in this place
that others convince me is my
home.

i sometimes even feel lost
in the path i've chosen to walk
down.

i often think,
will i always feel lost?

will i feel this way if i reach the
end?

maleeha ravat

i've learned to happily stay with
those who accept me
and not to settle
with those who tolerate me.

maleeha ravat

thank you,
for holding my hand.
when it still remembered,
all those times it was abandoned.

facing you,
i am proud.
that i finally gave myself
that one chance.

one chance
was all i needed.
to show you that
i didn't just fly,
i *soared*.

all the tears that
i spilled from my tired eyes
seem worth it.

now, that i can smile by myself.

maleeha ravat

it was tiring,
not physically but mentally.

why was i trying so hard
for people who had already given
up?

i saw your love,
in all the things you did for me.

when you were certain i wouldn't
leave,
you told me what i already knew.

maleeha ravat

holding on to what no longer
serves a purpose,
is like watering a dead plant.

your intentions may be good
but it's futile.

balance.

isn't that what we all want.

not too much,
but not any less.
enough to make us feel,
but not feel restless.

how silly it is
for us to think,
that we can experience
something so intricate
all the time.

maleeha ravat

in these moments that feel like
they'll never end.

will you stay with me?

will you hold me?

until i feel the peace,
that i currently crave for.

my mind is busy
with foggy thoughts.

some of them are worries,
which are strangely not even my
own.

whilst, some are situations,
that will never happen.

maleeha ravat

i was never quiet.
you just treated me,
the way you thought was best.

eventually, i just became your
shadow.

maleeha ravat

i was stuck in darkness.
for what, i thought would be
forever.
but, you came along.

then, i realised i just was
standing in a tunnel
and you, well you, were my light.

maleeha ravat

i am scared.

i can see my way out.
but, my feet don't seem to move.

i just remind myself,
that one small step is all it takes.

maleeha ravat

i stopped being who i truly was,
because of you.

so, who did you love?

me or the mask i wore to make
you stay?

maleeha ravat

i realised you didn't care,
when you smiled,
and i had to pretend i hadn't been
sobbing.

all the reasons you loved me
became all the reasons you hated
me.

did you change
or just reveal who you really
were?

maleeha ravat

i am scared to love
but with you,
i feel like i can.

maleeha ravat

you said, you didn't do much.
but you stayed.
not many have.

maleeha ravat

it has been hard for me lately.

i say i'm fine but i'm not.
i don't want to go out.
i want someone by my side.

we don't even need to talk.
let's just watch the shadows,
my desk lamp creates.
will you come?

i don't think you will come,
because it's not important to you.

it isn't something you can post
online.

so, i tell you to have fun with the
others going out,
and i sink further into my bed.

thinking back,
it was that day.

remember when we were
walking,
the path was quiet and our
giggles
were stupidly loud.
then, just like it was all written
perfectly,
it started to rain.

oh god, how i love you.

between shared stories
and nights staying up,
i knew i found what others called
destiny.

you just let me be for a while.
whether i am overwhelmed or
overjoyed.

you listen, stare and slowly begin
to speak.

i just know you were sent to me
by something greater than what's
between the two of us.

maleeha ravat

keeping up with you,
meant that i was running away
from me.

i don't want to run away from me
anymore.

if you dare to hide behind
what others believe
and hurt me.

at least, look me in the eyes
and say what others have told
you to say.

another year passes.

with every growing second,
time seems to escape
through the spaces of my fingers.

i don't fear time passing,
but i fear not living to the best of
my ability.

i often ask myself,
can i do better?
did i miss another opportunity?
or will i have the same amount of
freedom
that i do in this moment?

it's overwhelming, but i'll start
this journey.
slowly.
step by step.

until my reflection
is one that i completely accept.

what will follow will be hard.
but i know
it is possible.

the reflection i may find
contentment in,
others won't,
and that is okay.

that reflection is mine,
and so is this journey.

maleeha ravat

i like to think it's true,
that floating aimlessly
once in a while
will set my mind free
from all those unheard worries.

so like a butterfly,
i spread my wings
and move in harmony
with the summer breeze.

our story may not mean much to
you.

but it will stay in my heart,
as one of the memories
i treasure the most.

maleeha ravat

time has passed,
but our hearts still stay tangled
in the name of love.

we shall always coexist;
like the crashing waves on the
shore
and the golden sand it kisses.

not perfect together,
but rather harmonious and
beautiful.

maleeha ravat

do you still want me?
or the comfort that i brought you,
pretending to be someone
you needed to get better.

maleeha ravat

time can be healing,
but cruel and slow.
it hurts,
long and hard.

all i can do
right now,
in this existing moment
is wait.

wait for it to get better.

i hope to return to you,
and run in
endless fields of flowers
when i do.

maleeha ravat

nothing i did was fake,
so i don't feel like
i could've done more.

if you took whatever i could
give,
i just wonder,
why are you still dissatisfied?

loving you was
harder than i thought,
because you believed that
love was a weakness.

maleeha ravat

i hope your 'one day'
becomes your today.

maleeha ravat

your promises are soft.
they litter my skin.

just like your deep kisses
that brush over my hidden
freckles.

maleeha ravat

no words need to be said.

it's the middle of the night,
and the silent calmness it brings
is loud enough.

being happy is what i wish for,
but it's not my end goal.

happiness is an extreme.
happiness is an emotion,
that comes and goes.

how can i fixate on something
that is so temporary?

maleeha ravat

i have come to accept
just because it's hard
doesn't mean you'll fail.
and if you fail,
so what?

failure only lets you learn
what you didn't know
to begin with.

maleeha ravat

all the years i spent surviving
doesn't mean i am behind others.

it just means, that now,
i can truly live.

maleeha ravat

where do all these feelings come
from?
i don't like it.

when will they go?
i have been laying here for hours.

maleeha ravat

all the questions that bothered me
are still unanswered.

but they don't hurt me anymore,
because i no longer let them
or *you* have power over me.

i don't want to go back.

i am who i am today.

if i try to erase all the pain,
that would mean
i would have to erase everything
else too.

the truth is that hurt people hurt
people.
i don't want to continue this
cycle.
i won't turn cold like you.

i will heal and move on.

maleeha ravat

i don't want to move.

it hurts, from head to toe.

i know nothing will change,
if i stay like this.

i'm too tired,
i'll try tomorrow.

for now, i'll just close my eyes.

what i yearned to hear
but never did,
i tell myself now.

hearing i am loved.

hearing i am beautiful.

hearing i am doing the best i can,
gently reassures
both me and my inner child.

it hurt.

it hurt so bad.

what i learnt from that,
is that if i want to cry,
i should.

i should cry
because it is what i feel.

what i feel is valid.

what i feel will pass.

what i feel isn't crazy.

why did i hold on for so long?

you dressed up your lies
and called them love.

why did i believe you?

maleeha ravat

to go where i have to,
i need to go *through* it.

it will be the hardest part
yet the most rewarding.

after being your punching bag,
you let me know
you weren't mad at me.

in fact, you were mad at yourself.

you were angry
because you knew you could do
better.

maleeha ravat

i like that i'm strong.

but, i wish,
i was only strong
because i wanted to be
and not because
i needed to be.

i feel free.

i'm running with you.

our hands happily
grabbing each other
and the wind
joining us
on this run too.

it took me a long time
to live for me.

before, i would live
for smaller things
and then for others.

suddenly, one day,
out of the blue,
i realised i was living
for myself.

i did it.

maleeha ravat

being invisible to others,
meant all those around me
would be their true selves.

people scare me.

maybe, because my past
was snatched from me.

anything that made me nostalgic,
i clung on to.

in hope,
that it wouldn't be snatched from
me either.

maleeha ravat

i didn't think
you could teach me anything.
but you did.

our pain brought us closer
together.

it wasn't supposed
to be a competition.

however, it turned
out that way.

because of that, i never spoke
and pulled up my sleeves.
so, my scars weren't visible.

maleeha ravat

you did your best,
but you still hurt me.

you don't even want
to acknowledge
how it all went wrong
or apologise.

please leave me alone.

you say being alone is weird.
but, i find some beauty
in that time away from others.

maleeha ravat

let's not worry too much
over what we can't control.

let's just do what we can,
with what we have
now.

Printed in Great Britain
by Amazon